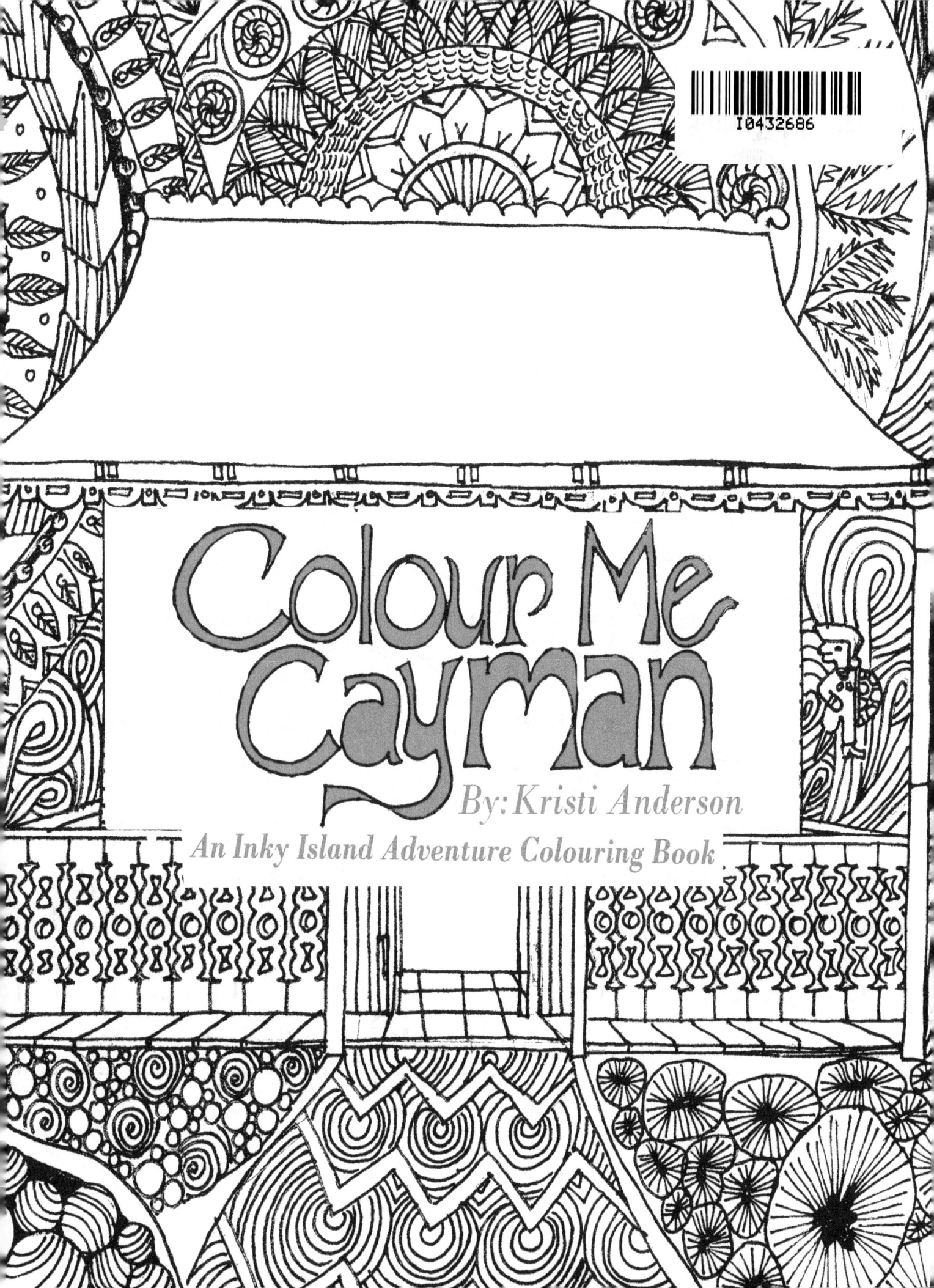

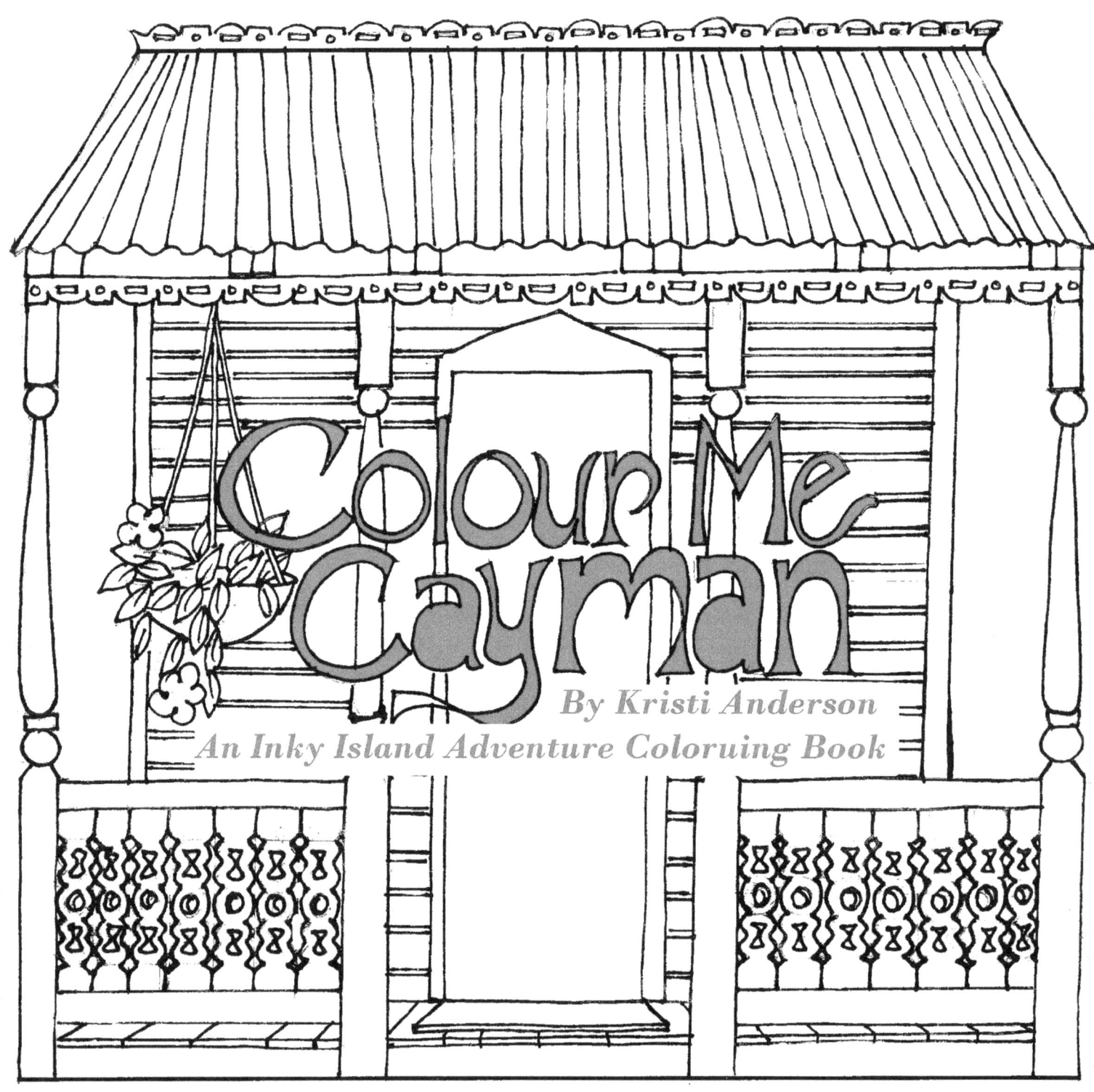

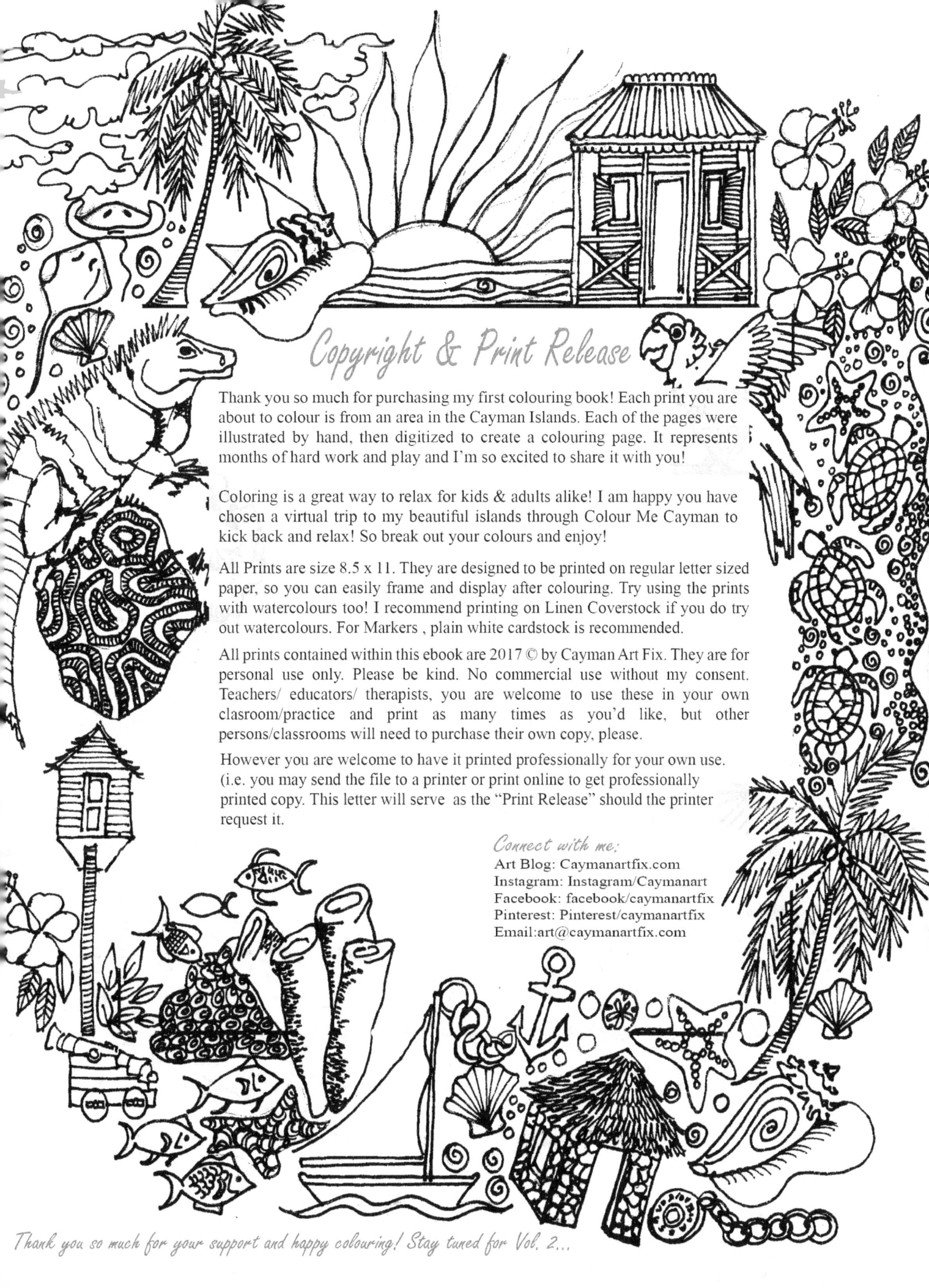

Copyright & Print Release

Thank you so much for purchasing my first colouring book! Each print you are about to colour is from an area in the Cayman Islands. Each of the pages were illustrated by hand, then digitized to create a colouring page. It represents months of hard work and play and I'm so excited to share it with you!

Coloring is a great way to relax for kids & adults alike! I am happy you have chosen a virtual trip to my beautiful islands through Colour Me Cayman to kick back and relax! So break out your colours and enjoy!

All Prints are size 8.5 x 11. They are designed to be printed on regular letter sized paper, so you can easily frame and display after colouring. Try using the prints with watercolours too! I recommend printing on Linen Coverstock if you do try out watercolours. For Markers, plain white cardstock is recommended.

All prints contained within this ebook are 2017 © by Cayman Art Fix. They are for personal use only. Please be kind. No commercial use without my consent. Teachers/ educators/ therapists, you are welcome to use these in your own clasroom/practice and print as many times as you'd like, but other persons/classrooms will need to purchase their own copy, please.

However you are welcome to have it printed professionally for your own use. (i.e. you may send the file to a printer or print online to get professionally printed copy. This letter will serve as the "Print Release" should the printer request it.

Connect with me:
Art Blog: Caymanartfix.com
Instagram: Instagram/Caymanart
Facebook: facebook/caymanartfix
Pinterest: Pinterest/caymanartfix
Email: art@caymanartfix.com

Thank you so much for your support and happy colouring! Stay tuned for Vol. 2...

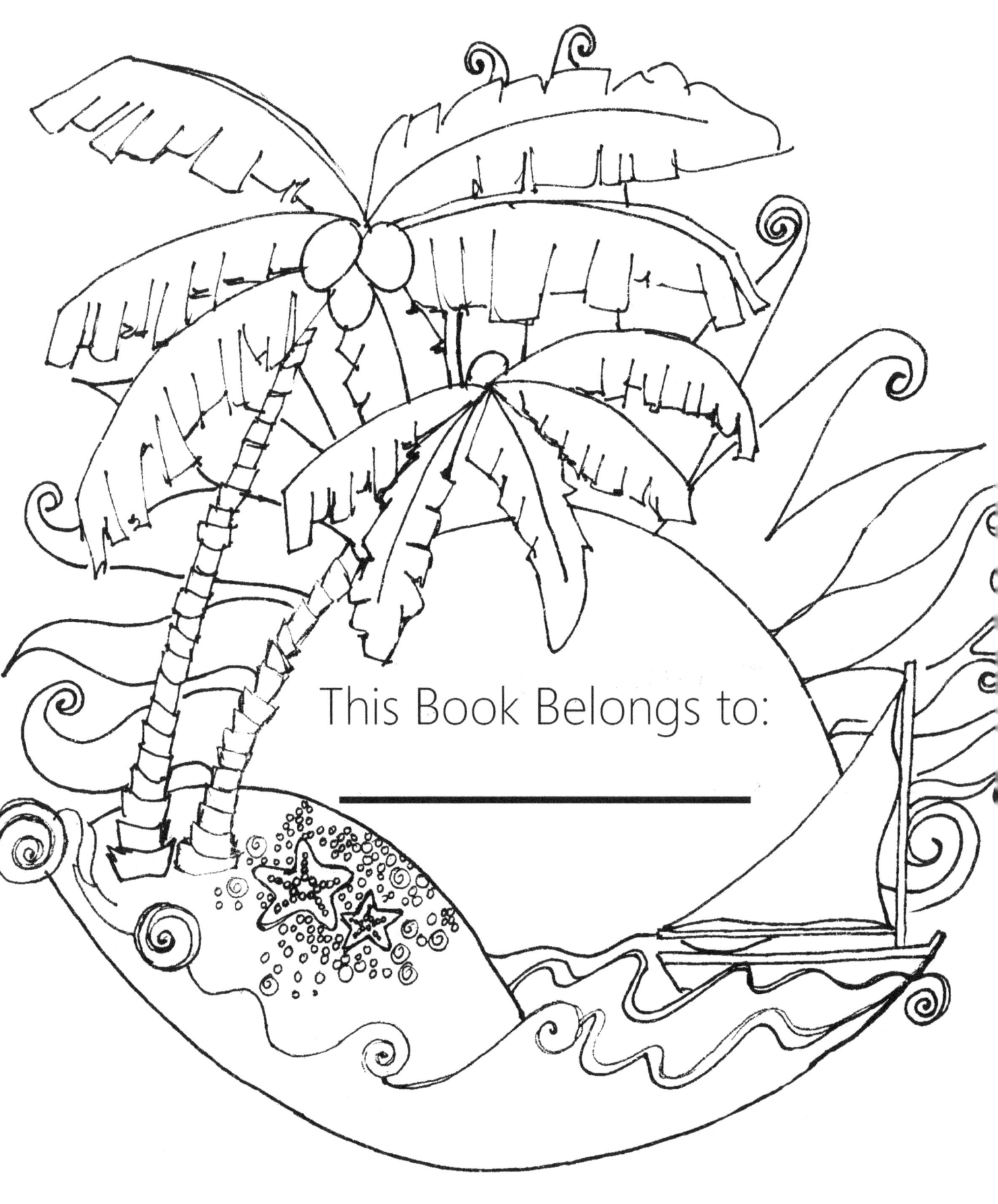

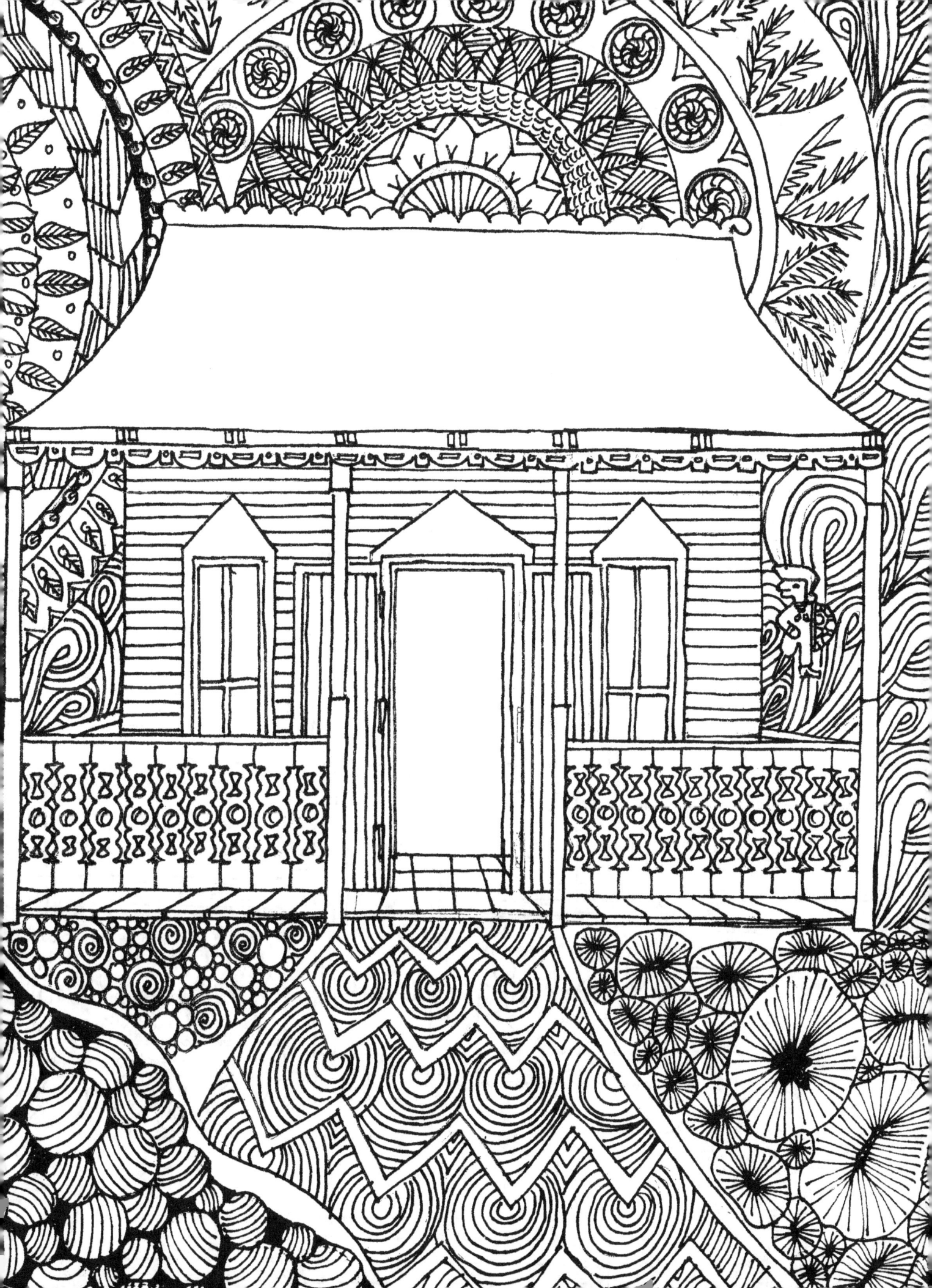

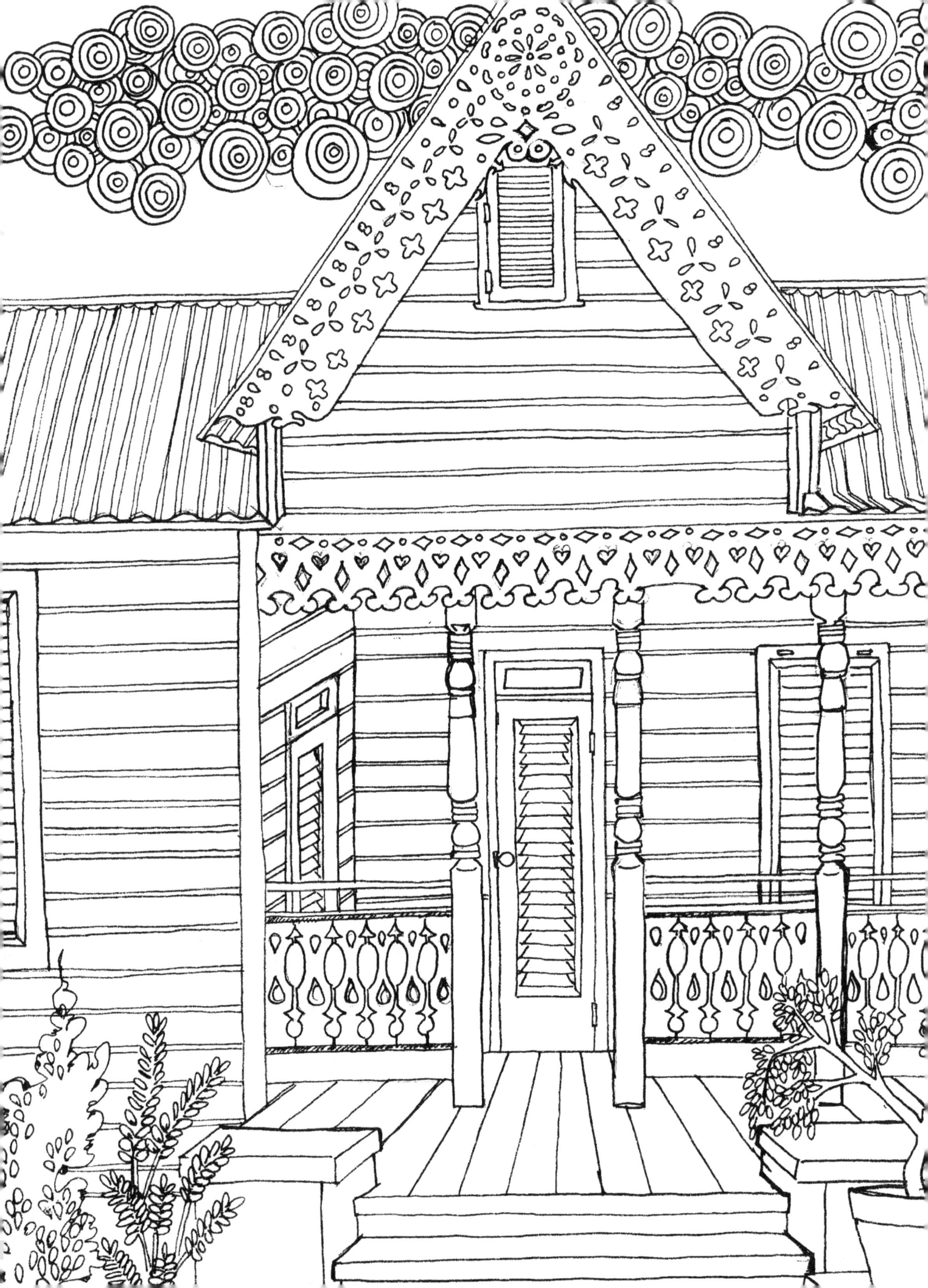

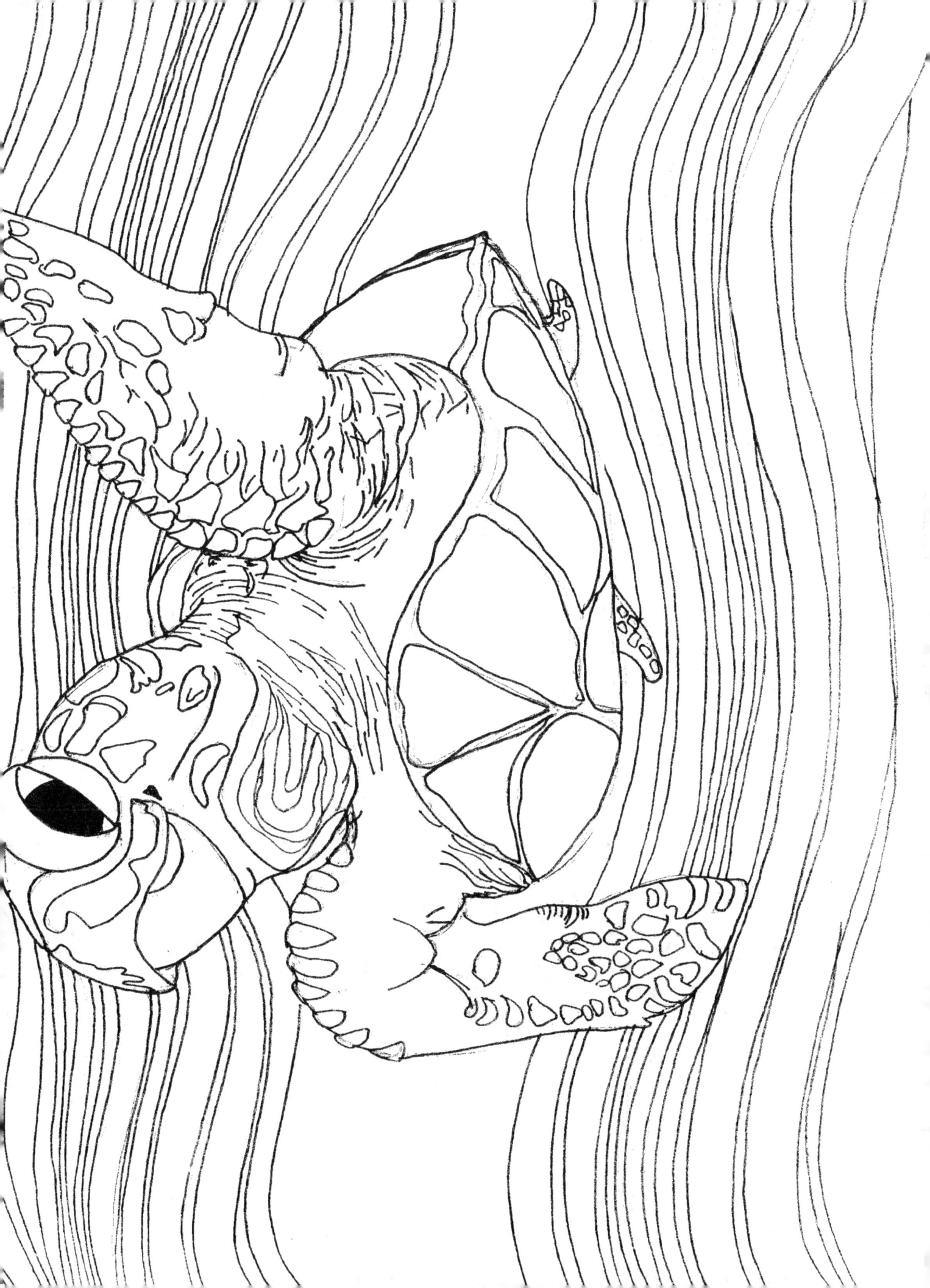

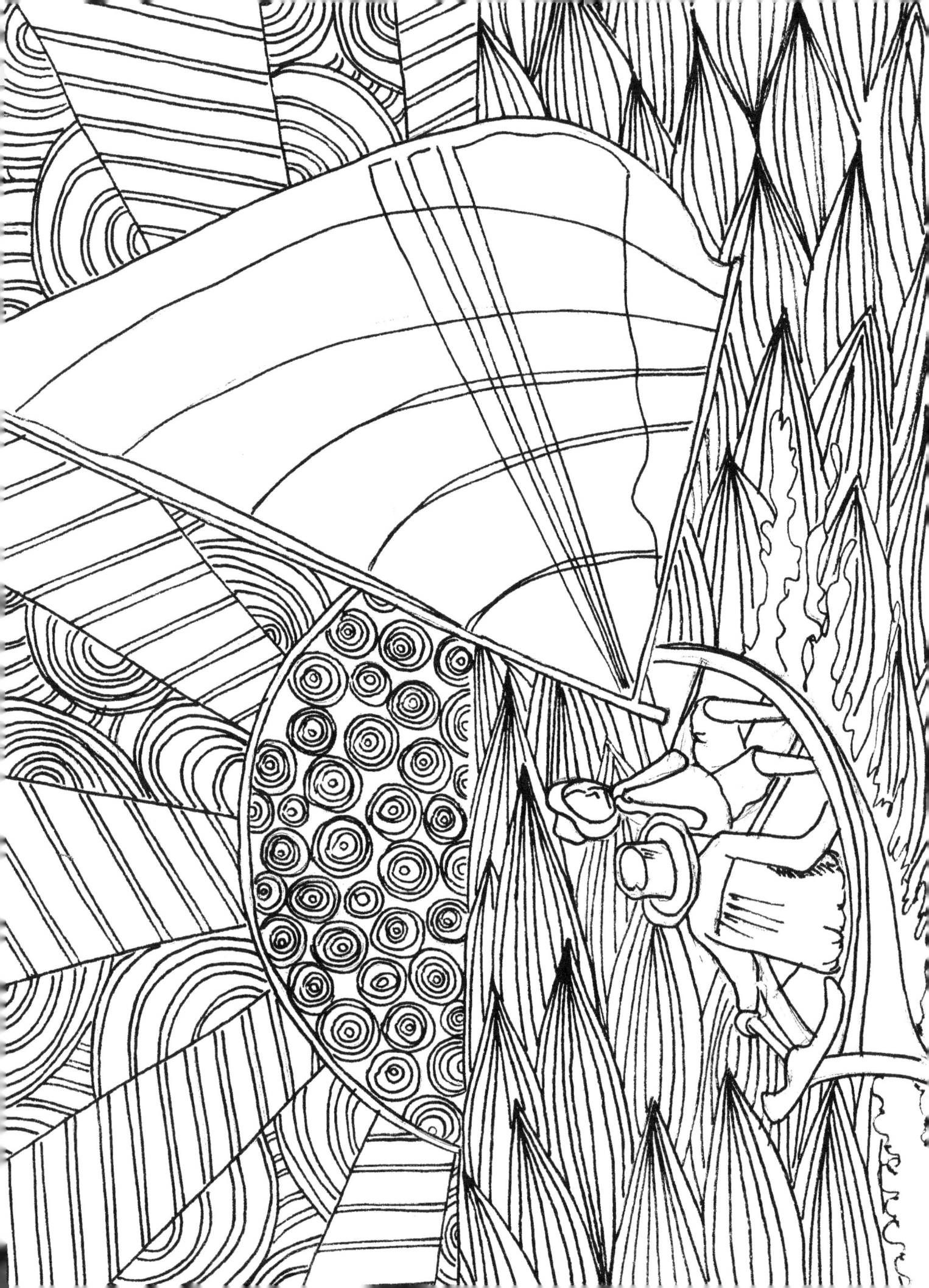

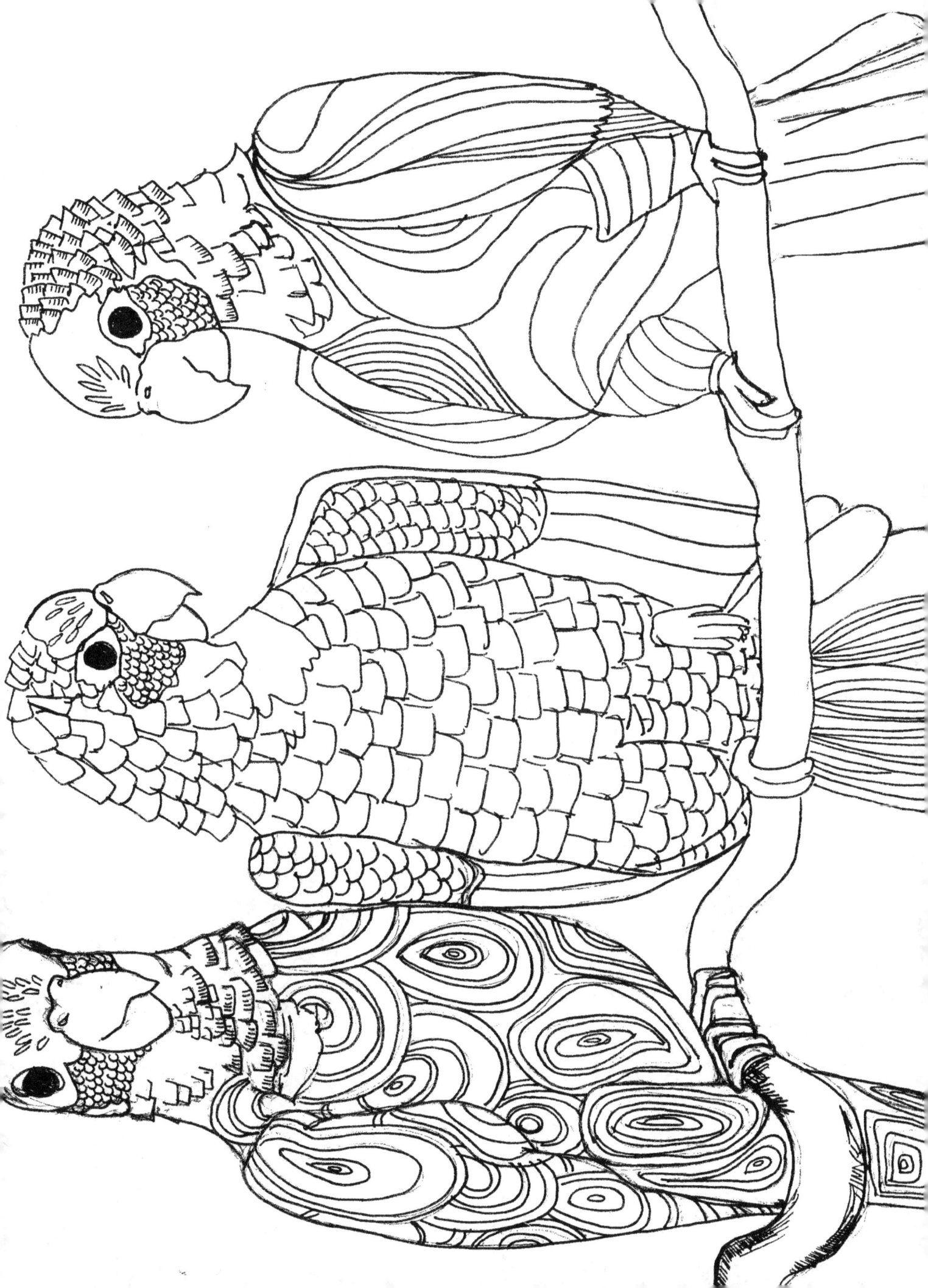

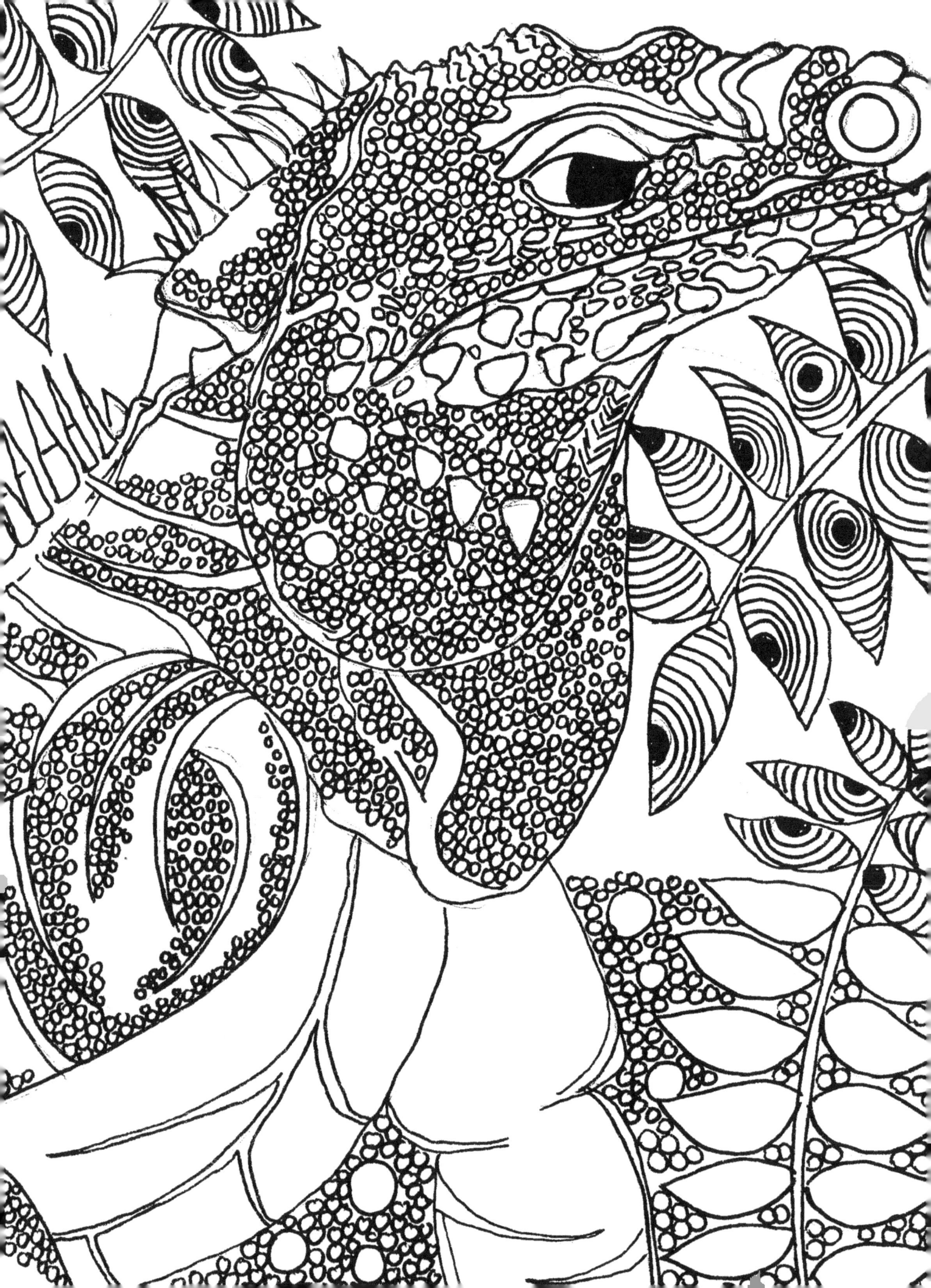

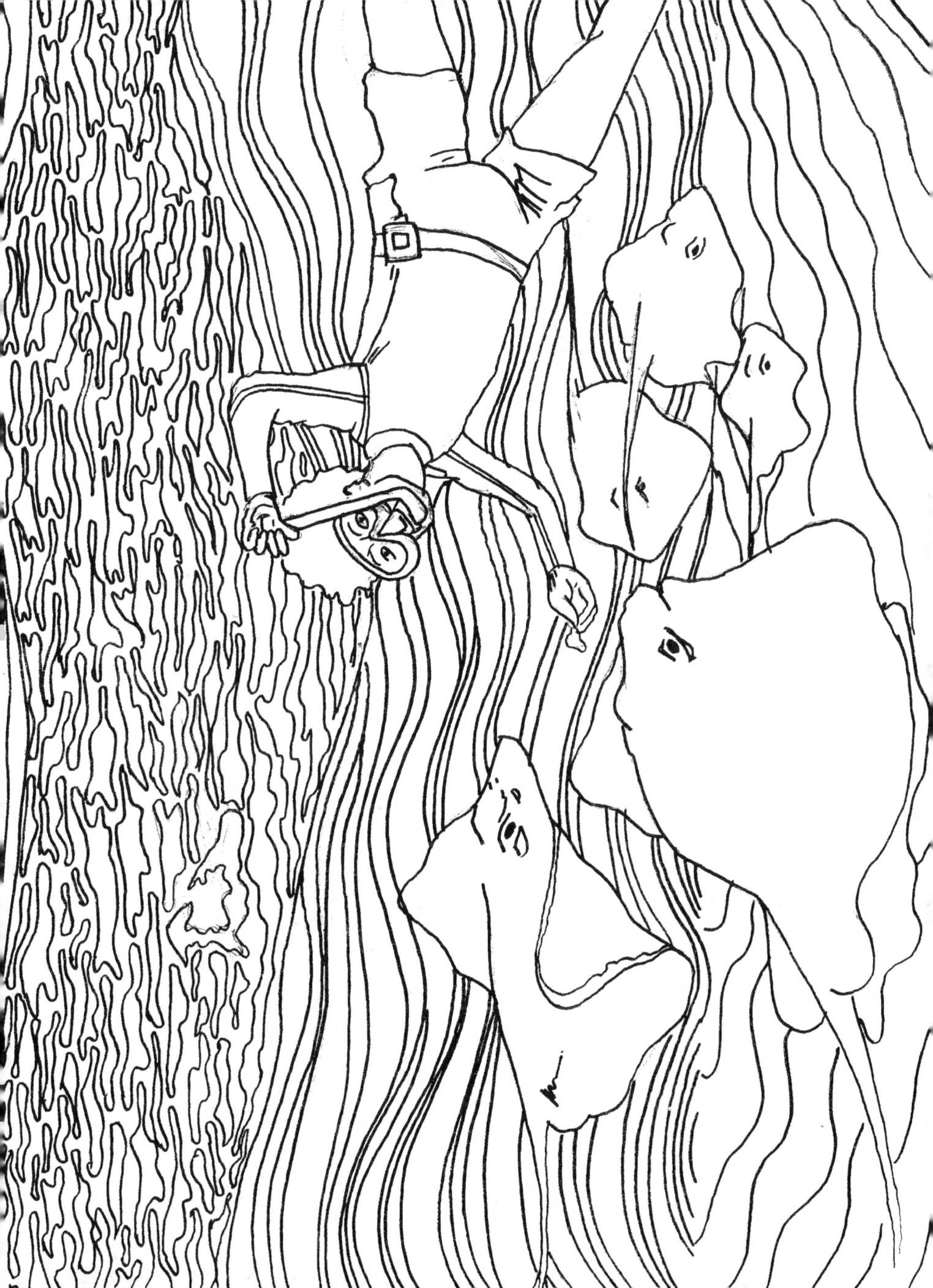

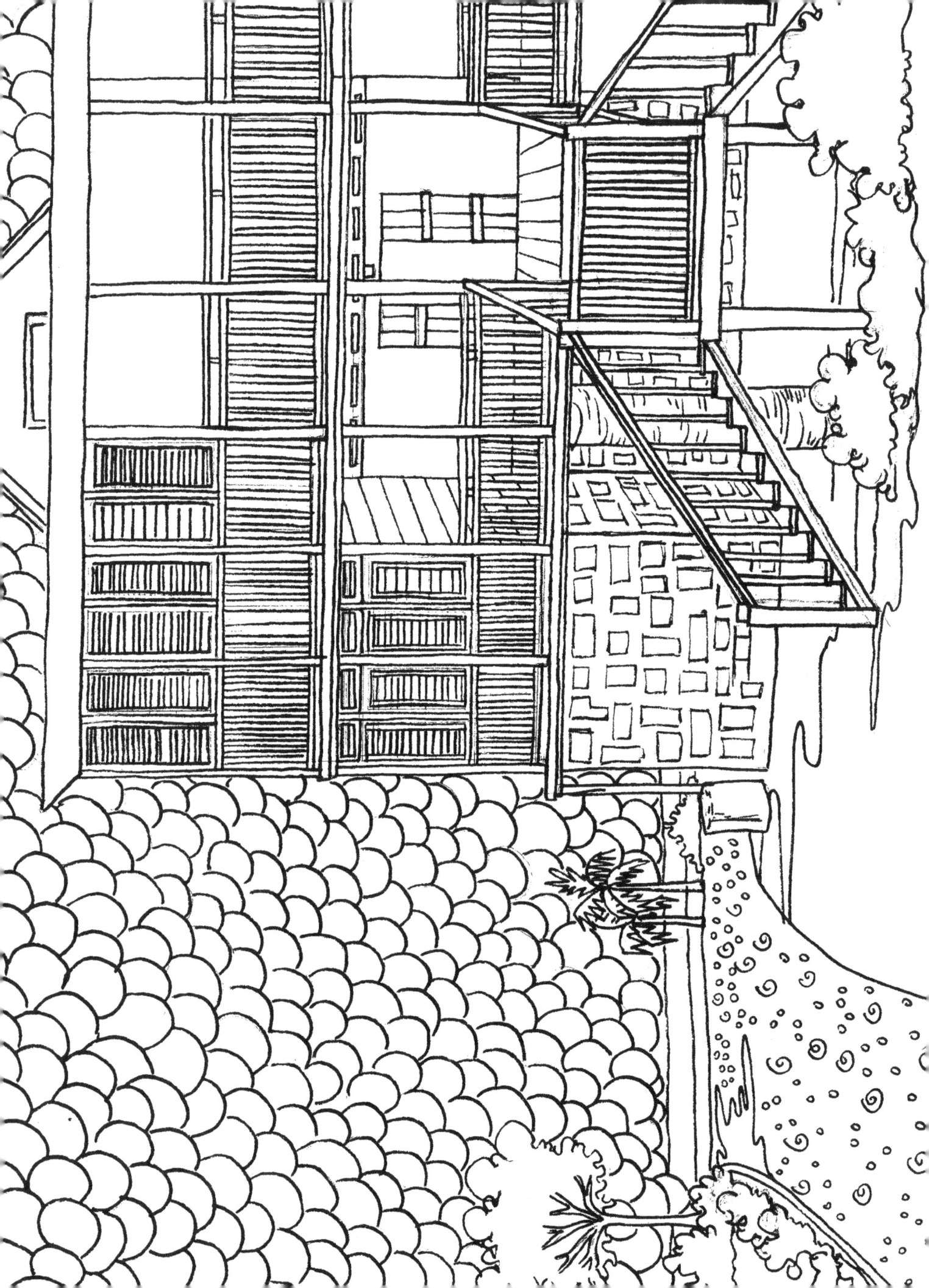

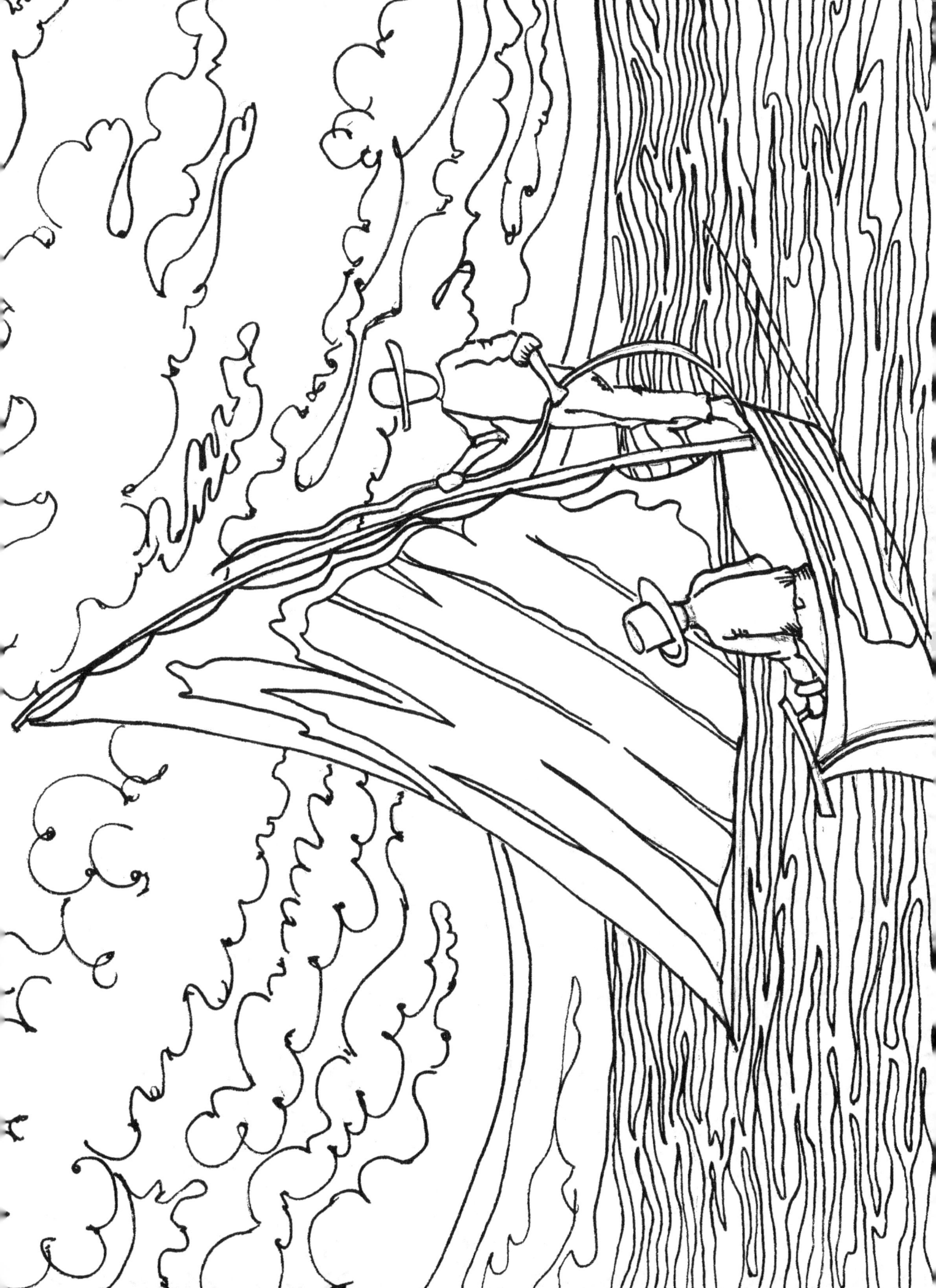

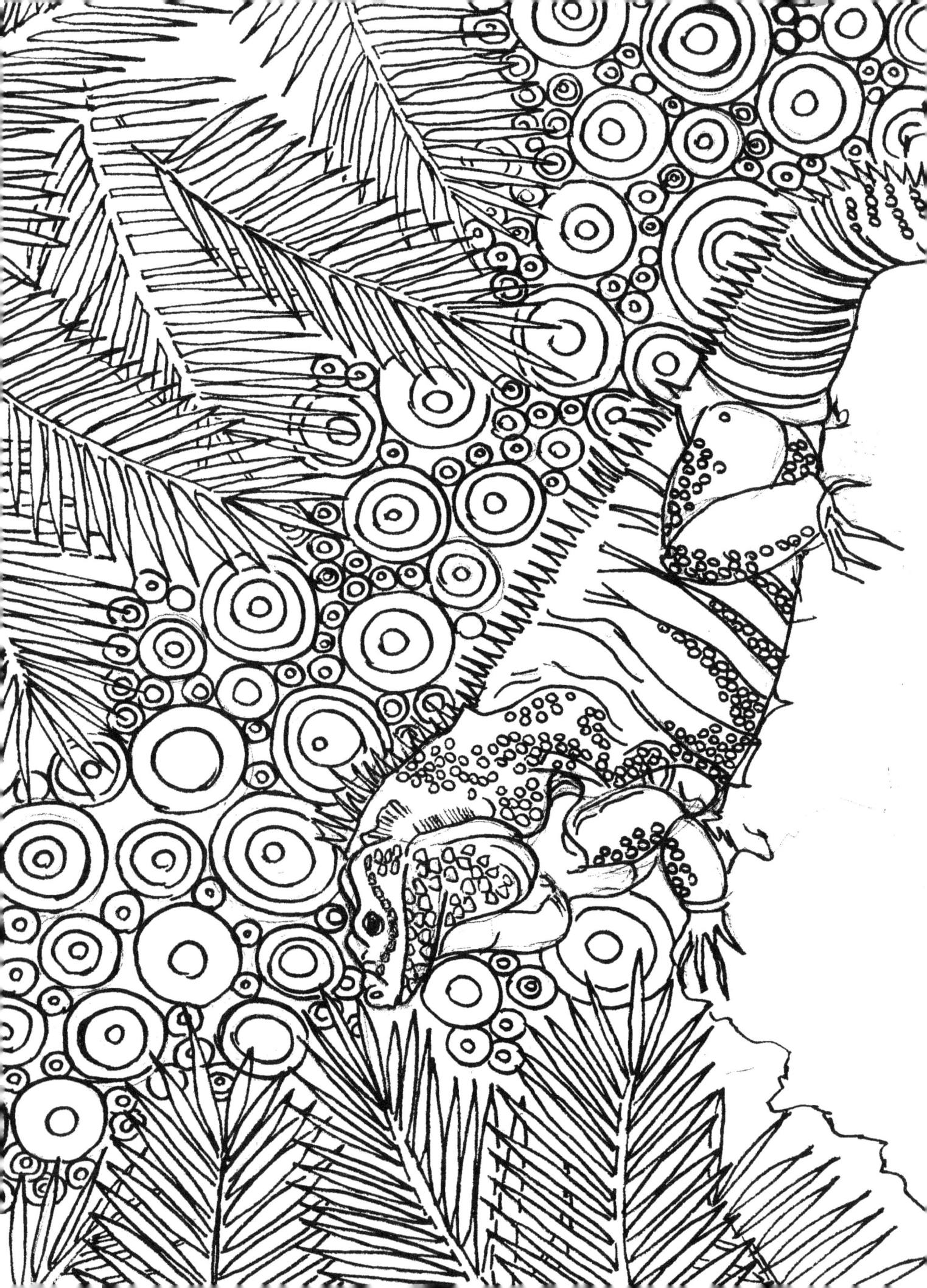

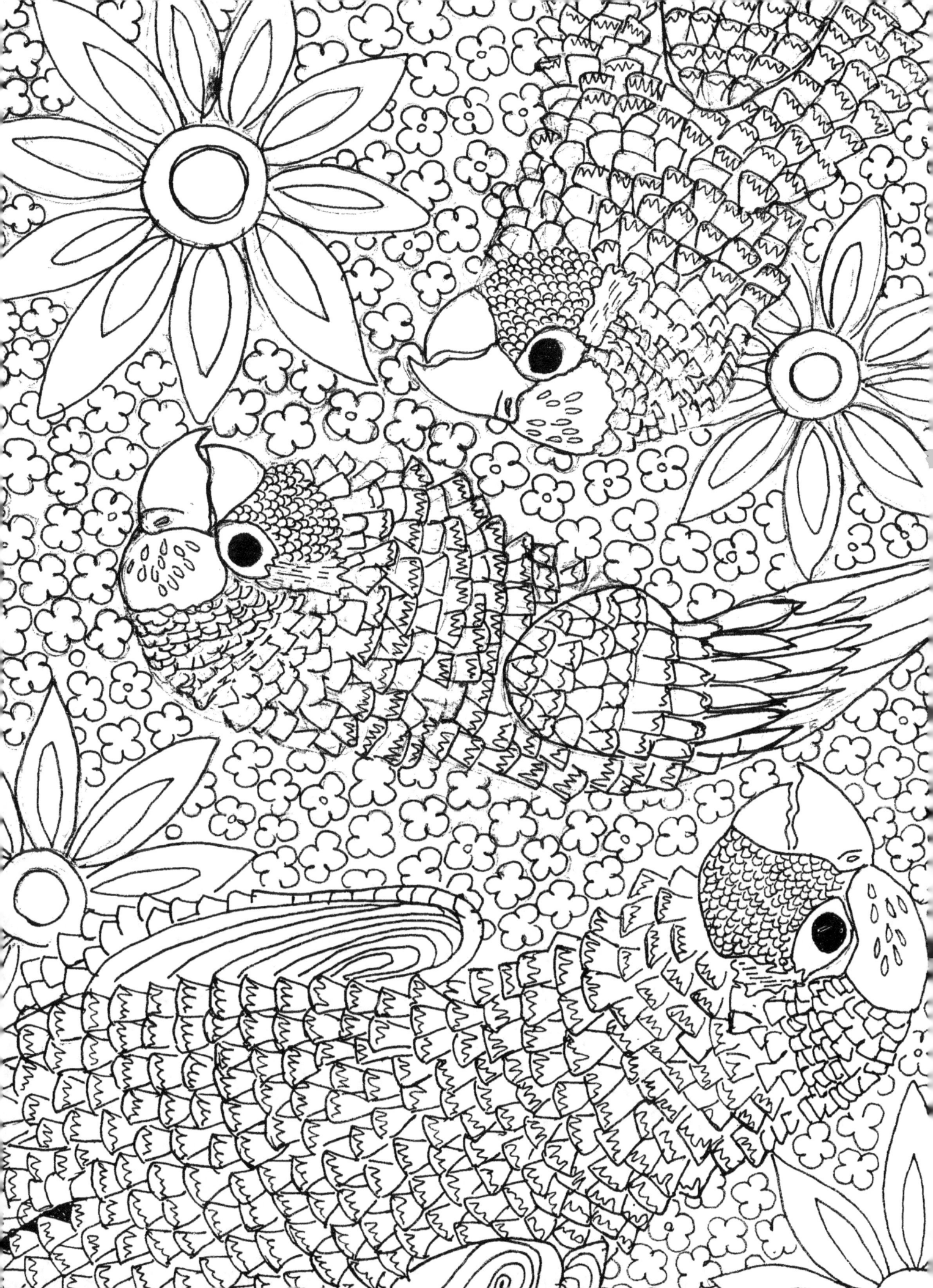

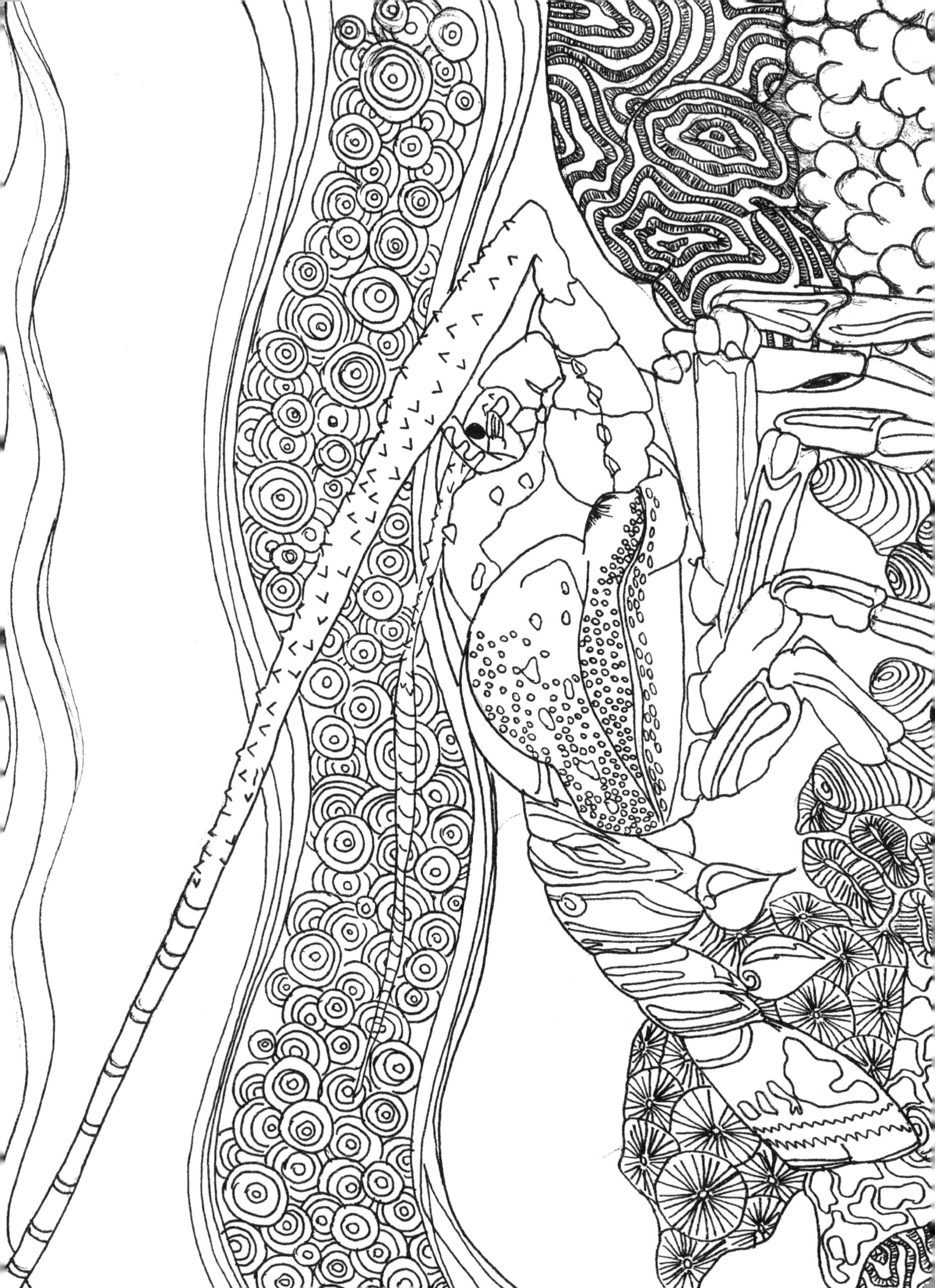

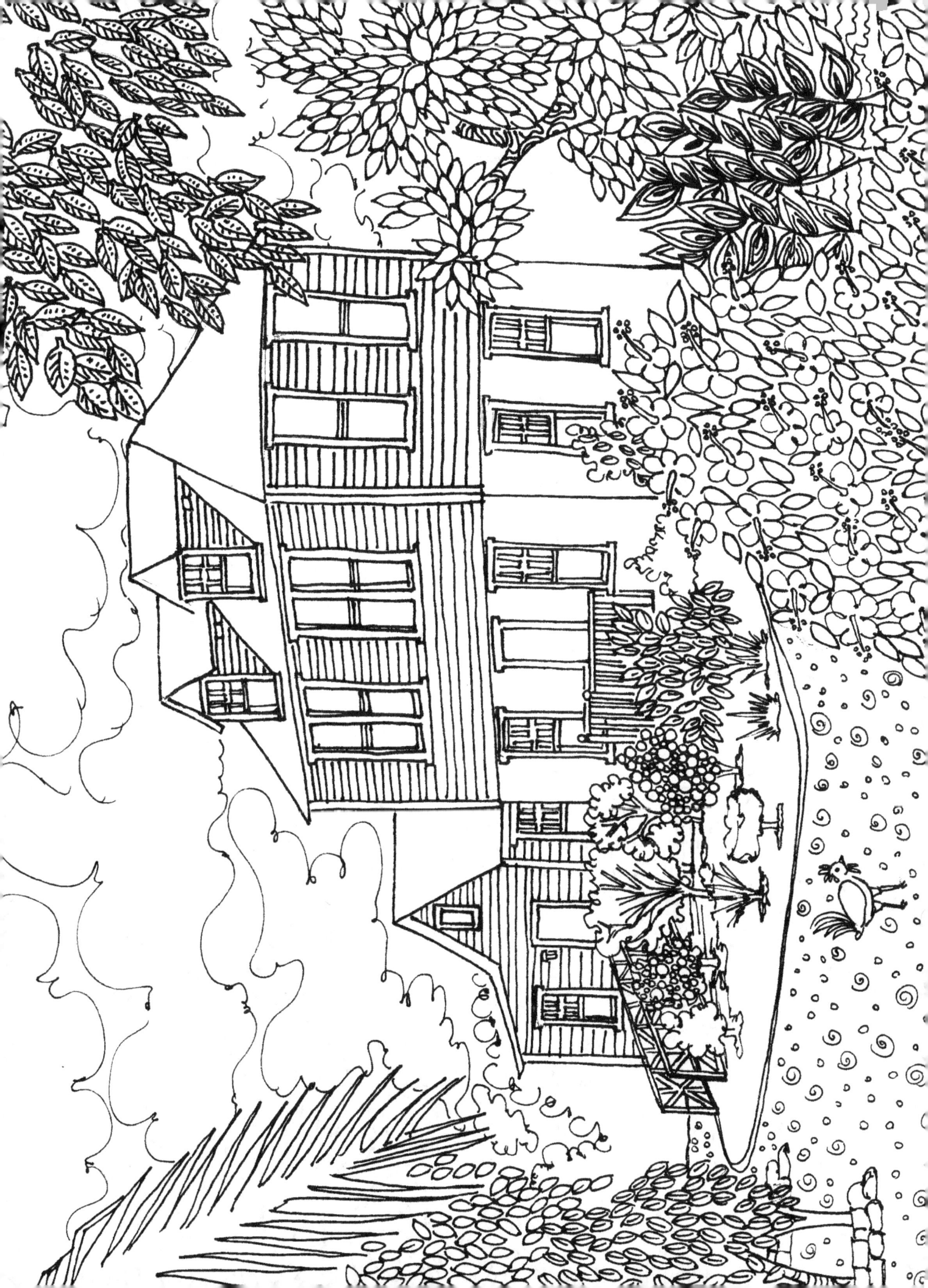

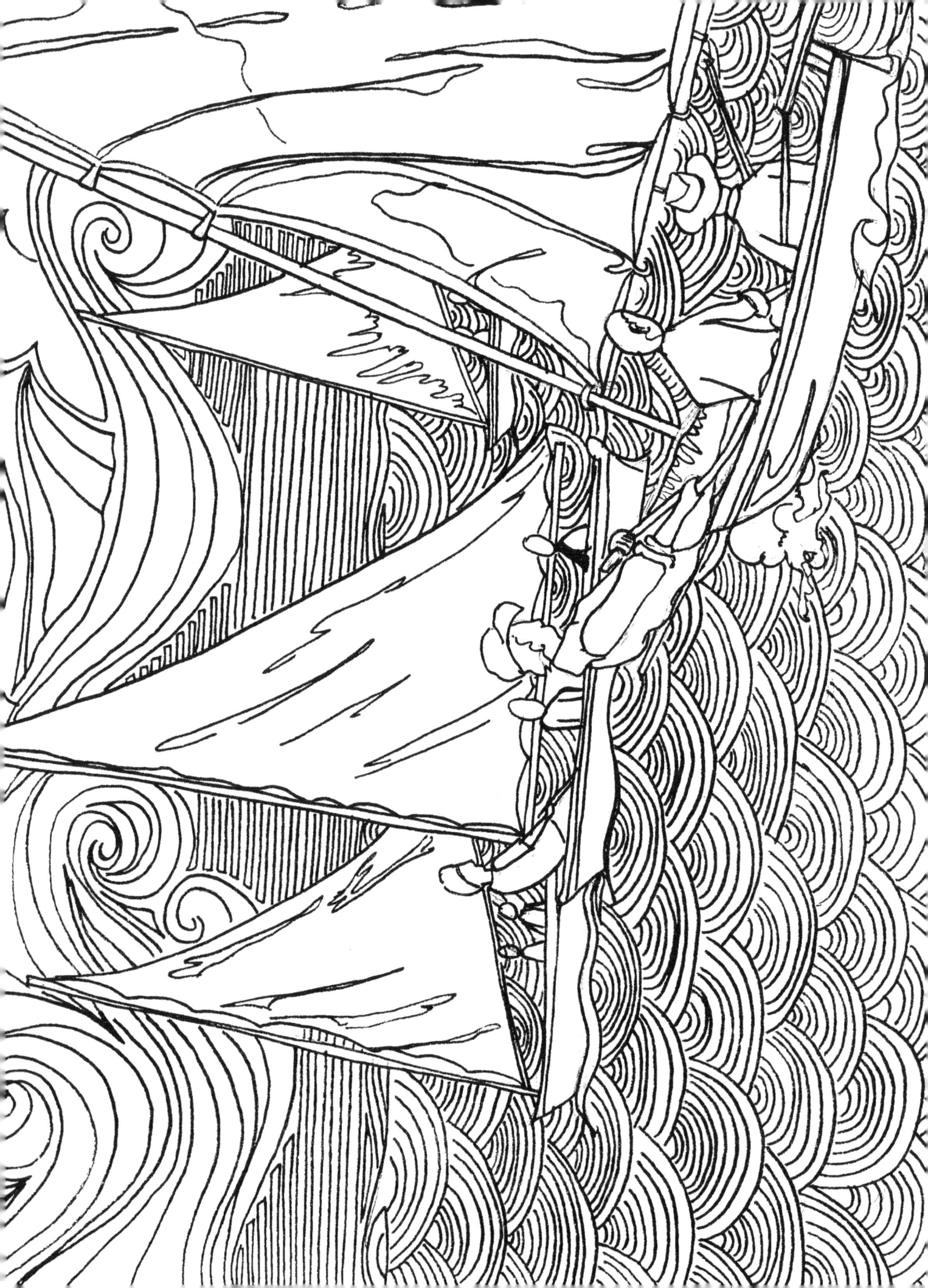

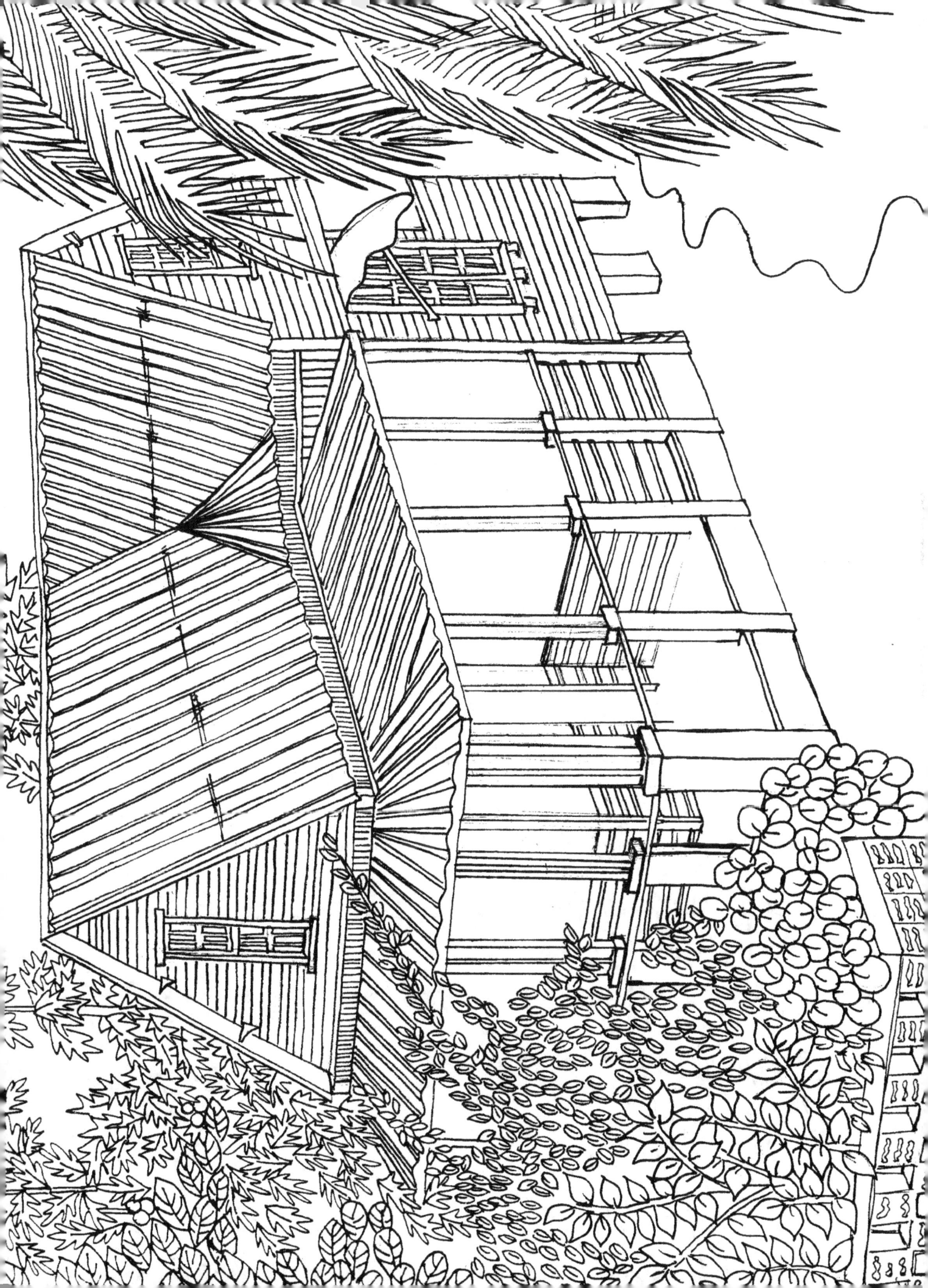

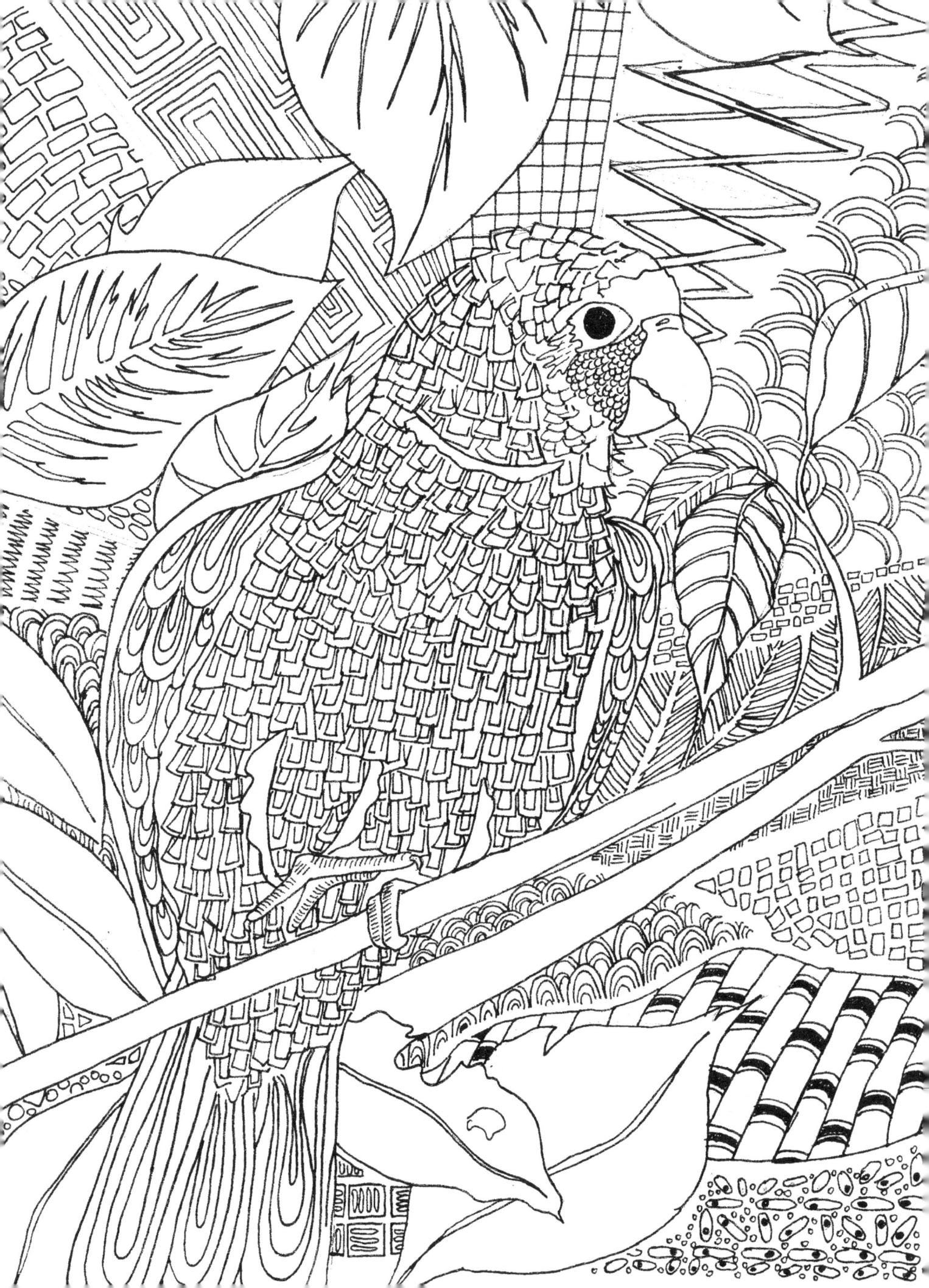

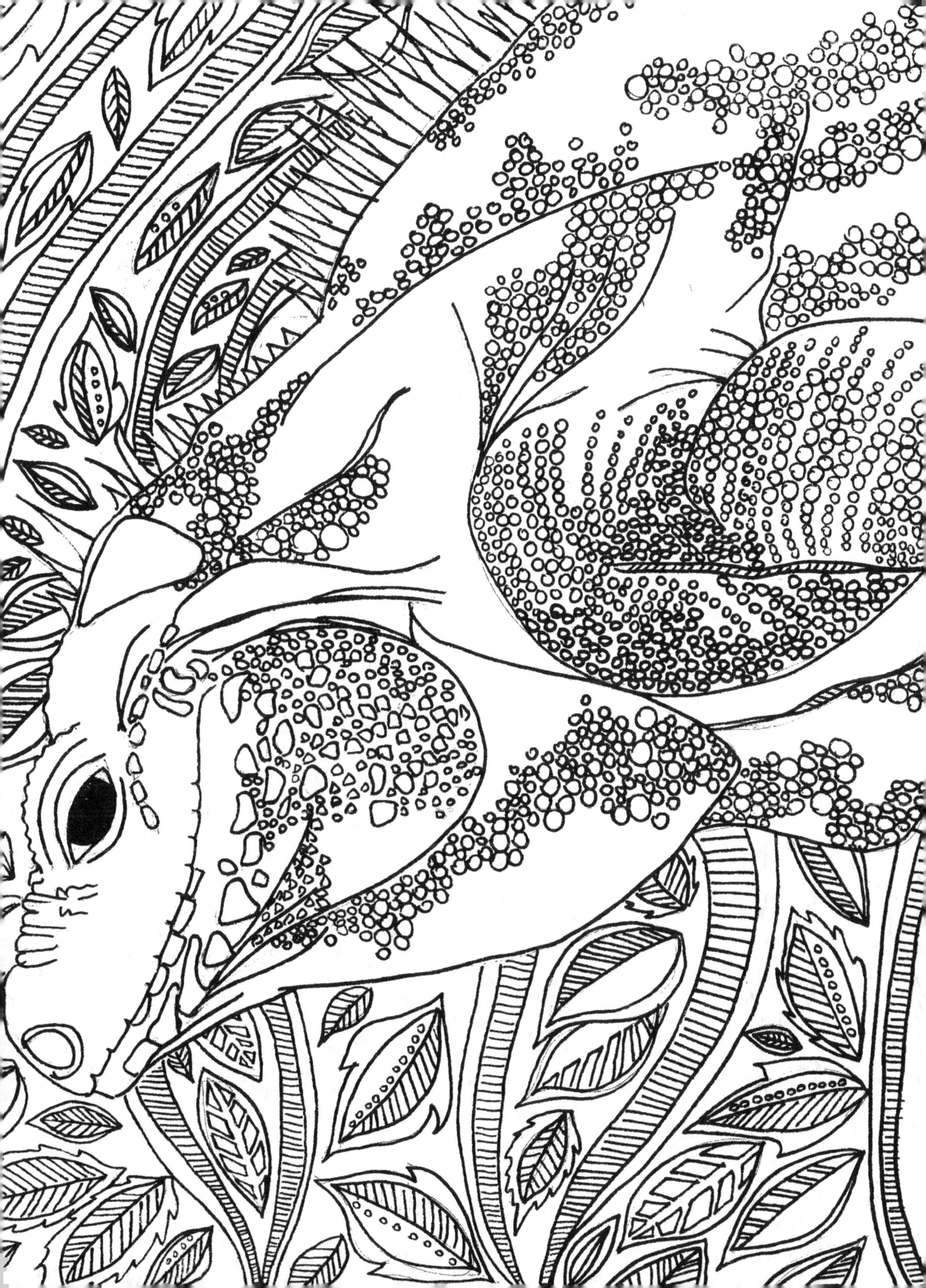

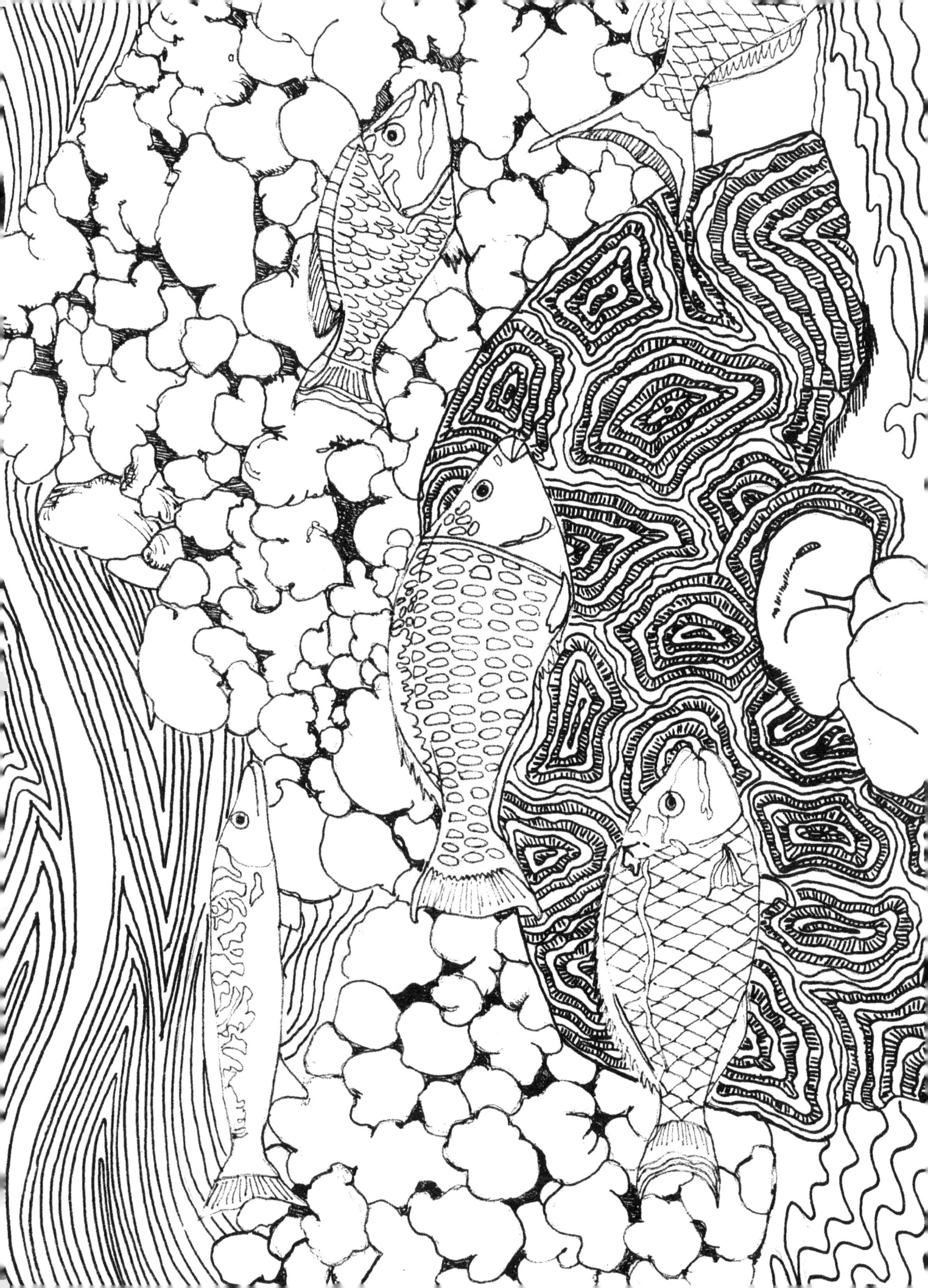

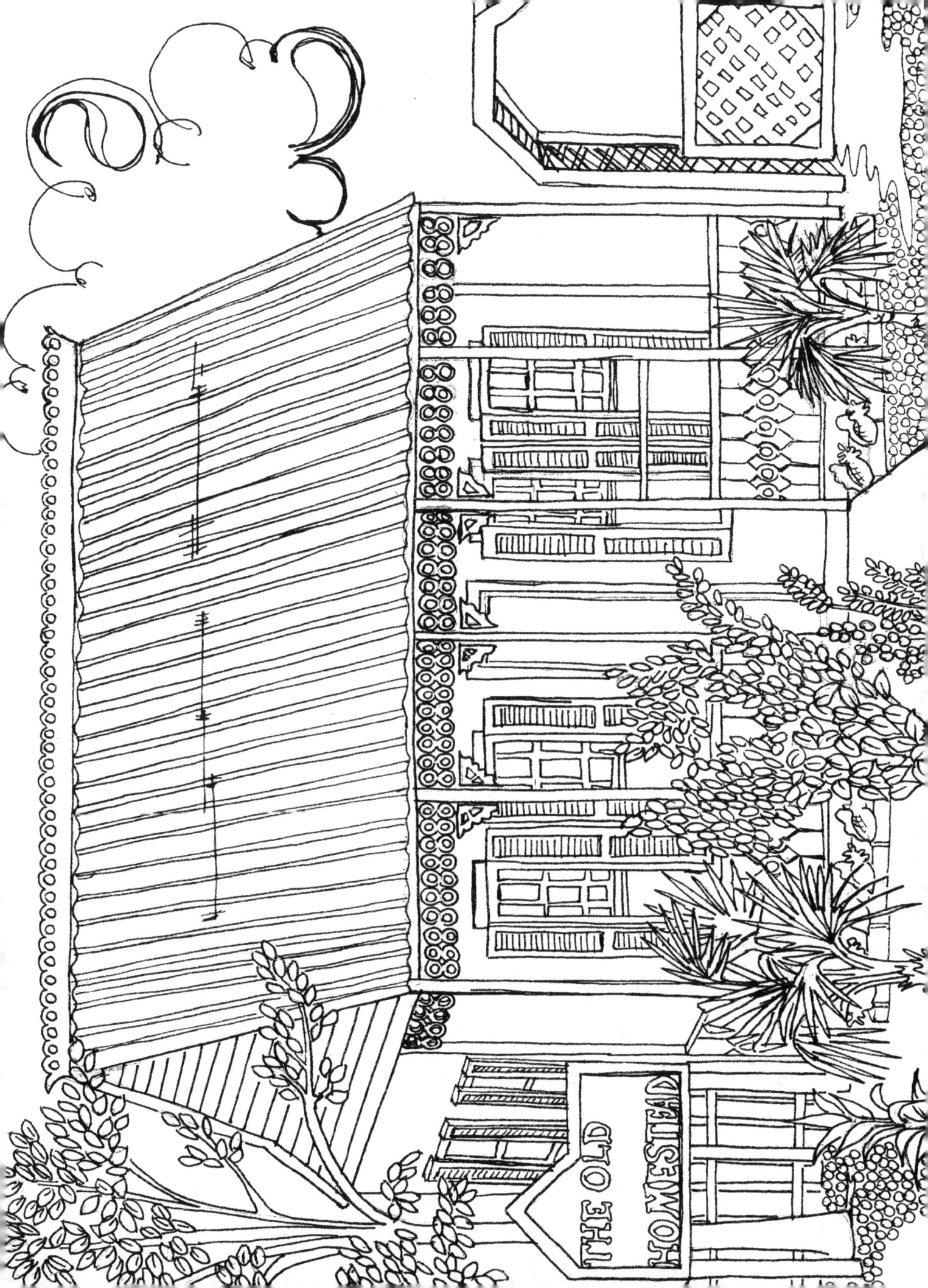

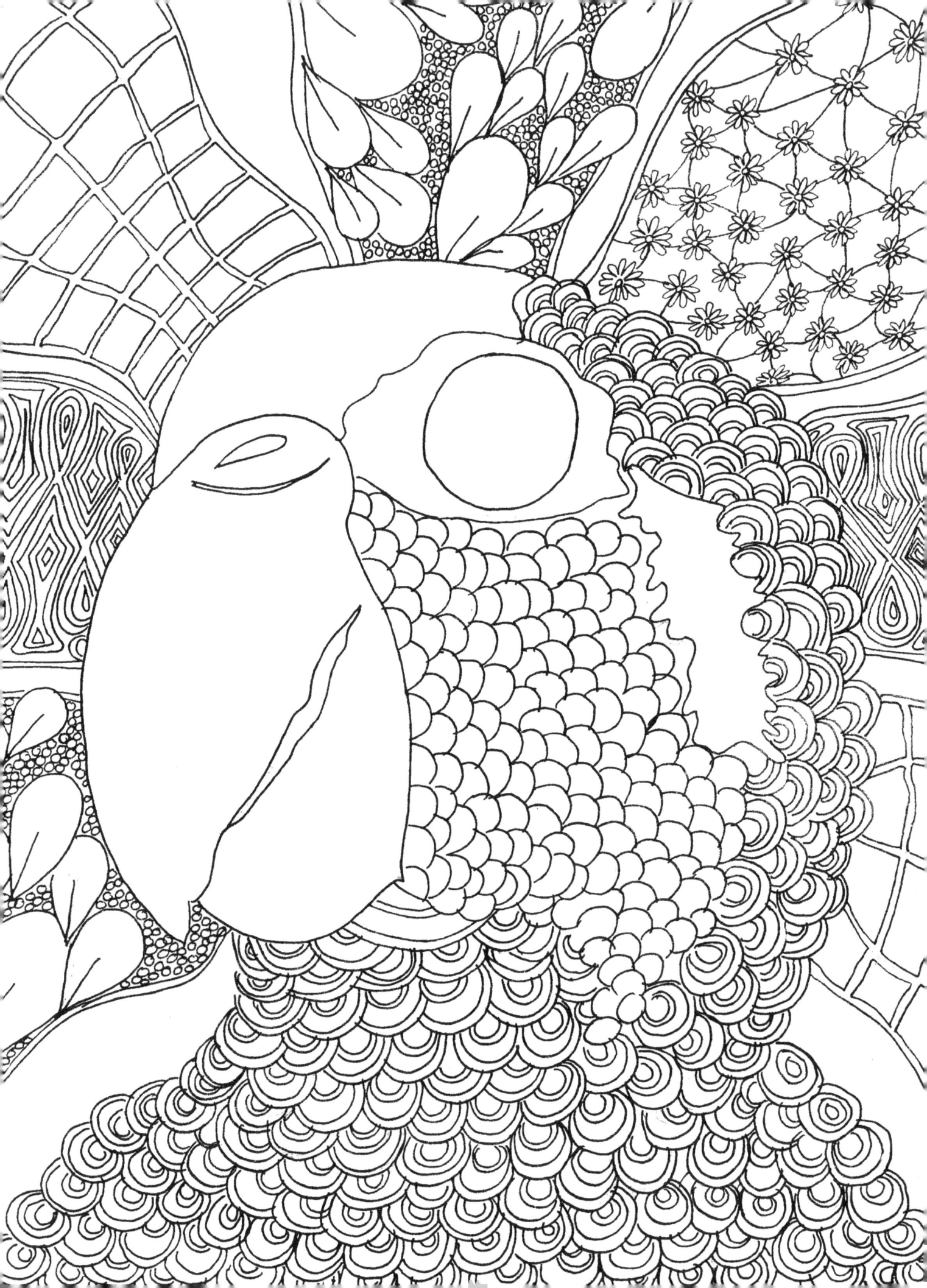

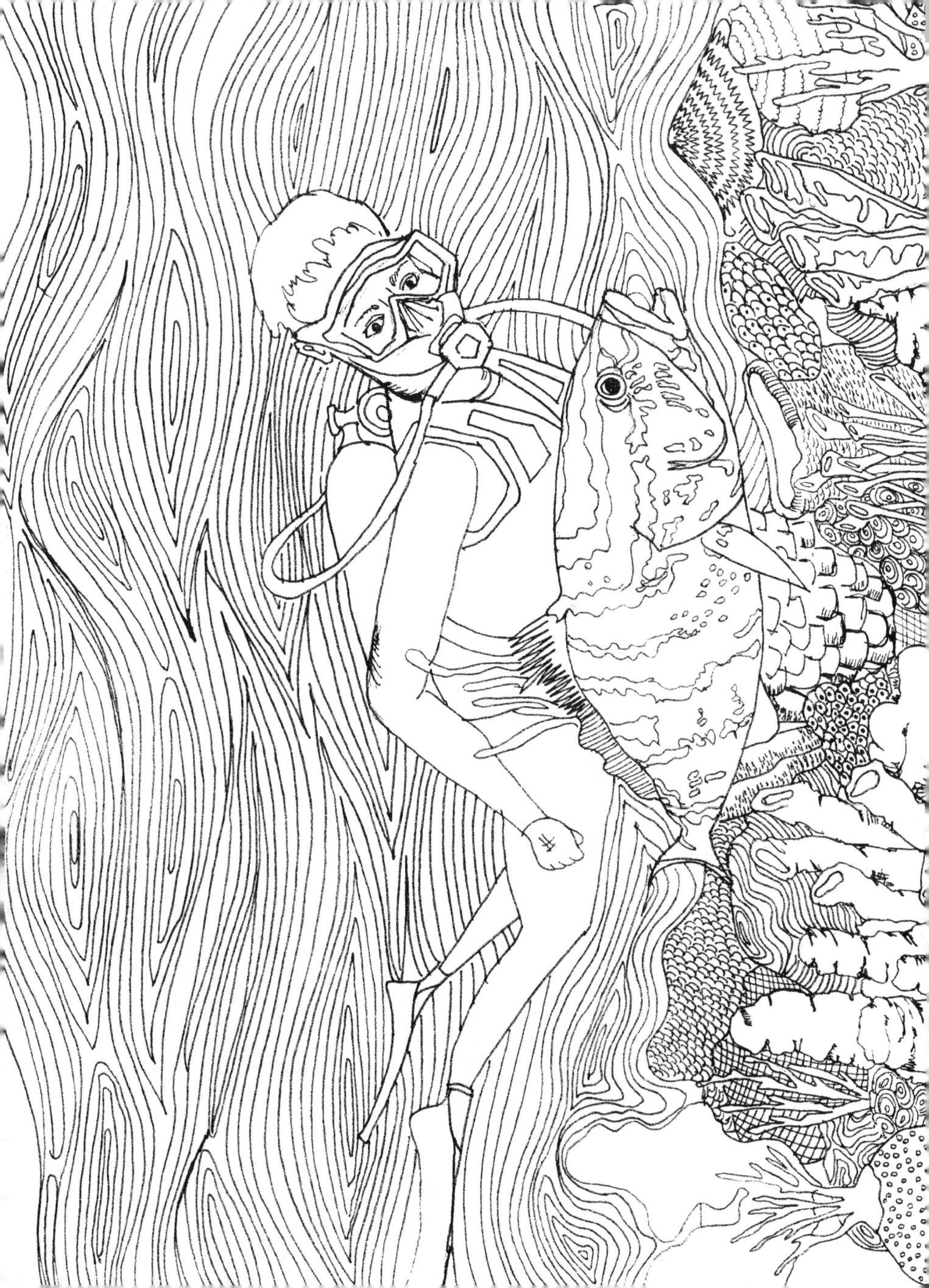

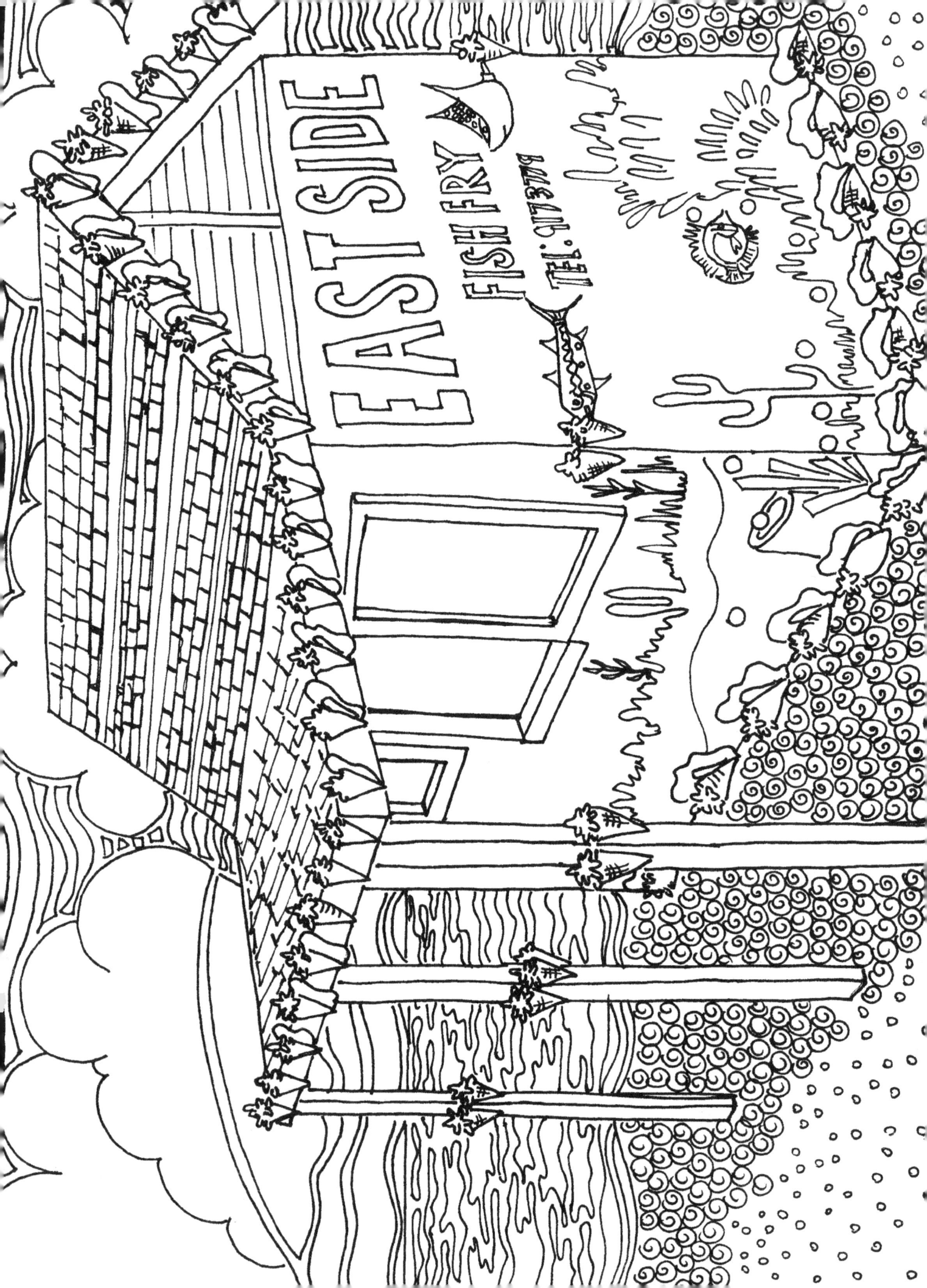

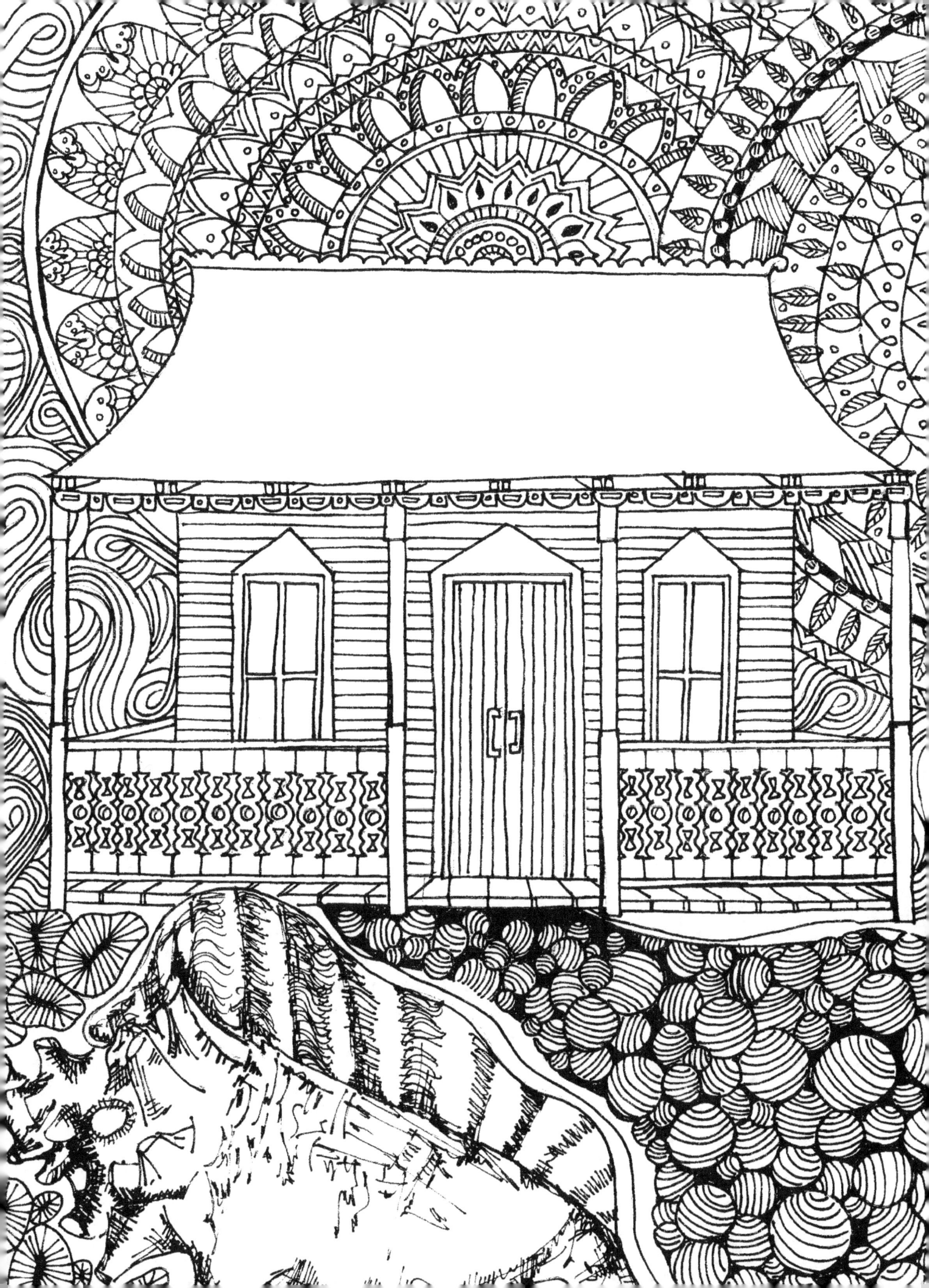

www.ingramcontent.com/pod-product-compliance
Lightning Source LLC
Chambersburg PA
CBHW062209220526
45470CB00009B/2983